How To Write Your Story

record your personal history in 30 minutes a day

Deb Graham

How To Write Your Story

record your personal history in 30 minutes a day

copyright 2014   Deb Graham

Other Books By Deb Graham:

Tips From The Cruise Addict's Wife

*Whether you are an experienced cruiser, or in the dreaming-about-it stage, you'll enjoy **Tips From The Cruise Addict's Wife**. Besides being crammed with more tips and hints than you'll find anywhere else, including how to save money, be the smartest passenger on any ship, and plan a great vacation, this acclaimed book is loaded with tips and stories that will have you laughing aloud.*

How To Complain...and get what you deserve

A customer's guide to complaining effectively in this day and age when customers feel like the low man on the totem pole.

Quick and Clever Kids' Crafts

Loaded with easy, classy crafts for children and adults. A must for parents, teachers, scout leaders and anyone else who'd rather see a creative child than a bored one

Awesome Science Experiments for Kids

Simple, impressive science experiments; a fun teaching tool for adults to share with kids

Savory Mug Cooking

Easy-yet-impressive lunch recipes made with fresh ingredients, cooked right in your favorite mug! Expensive Take Out lunches—not anymore!

Uncommon Household Tips

Use ordinary items in extraordinary ways

Dozens of new uses for twenty ordinary household items you don't think twice about. From using golf tees to hang your hammer to dental floss for scrapbooking, you'll be inspired to look around the house before you run back to the store.

How To Write Your Story

record your personal history in 30 minutes a day

Deb Graham

Why Write Your Own Story?

It's a scary thought--What if you died before you told your life's story, and your busybody sister-in-law decided to write it for you? Yes, she's diligent, but she never really liked you, and she surely doesn't know you as well as you know yourself. No one can tell your life's story as clearly or as accurately as you can! Now's the time, before it's too late.

In only thirty short minutes a day, you can begin to tell your own history, drawn from your own memories. Thousands of people have done this, and found it compelling, even addictive. This short book makes it easy, with dozens of questions and memory-prompts, carefully designed to get you thinking, to aim your mind in a direction to record your own life history. As you begin, it's as easy as any essay test you've ever taken. Easier, because you know the subject matter intimately---it's about YOU.

Telling your story has more benefits than you can see! One, of course, is that your legacy will be honest and accurate, built from your own experiences, from your own viewpoint, not cobbled together by generations to come. Think what a treasure it would be for you to come upon your great-great-grandmother's handwritten story, in her own words, in her own timeframe! Do you owe that gift to your own future posterity? Just think—the everyday wisdom now disdained by your teenagers will be cherished in years to come....*but only if you write it down now.*

The world is changing fast! Politically, socially, technologically, militarily, morally; it's changing at breakneck speed. In your life, you have already seen many changes and innovations. Things that seem miraculous to us now will be commonplace to generations to come. Things we see as ordinary will be as archaic as ice boxes and horse drawn carts to our future families! Begin now to record your day to day point of view.

There is great power in words! Wrapping words around thoughts makes them more solid. Putting feelings and thoughts into words can make them more real, more tangible.

Any decent therapist worth the price will invariably tell you to write your feelings. They may suggest a mind map, or a journal, or a list; some even provide fill-in-the blank forms. After you pry words out of your brain and out the end of your finger, you can objectively look at them. The very act of writing can change who you are, simply by allowing you to see yourSelf.

As you write, you will begin to see yourself in a different light. You may identify patterns and strengths that had been overlooked, character traits you had buried, talents you had not noticed. As you scrawl your thoughts and memories you thought you had forgotten, you will gain a broader sense of your Self. And it's cheaper than therapy or a life coach!

Plus, looking back over your story, you'll be able to see patterns that you would otherwise miss. It'll open insights that can be a huge benefit to you now, as well as leaving a legacy for those who come after you.

Our society moves at breakneck pace, with demands upon our time varied and constant. We are barraged with noise and stimuli that can sap our spirit, and even cause physical symptoms. Many doctors recommend taking time to relax, and have a quiet time, free from technology and noise. Quietly carving out time to write is certainly valuable, in more ways than you can immediately see!

As you develop the habit of writing a few minutes each day, you will find yourself calming, automatically slipping into a less frenzied mindset. Your mind will anticipate today's question, and you'll find yourself mentally relaxing as you reach for pen and paper.

Don't let any excuses get in your way. Now's your time to tell your story! This is a project for which you have already done the research, simply by living your life.

Overcoming Objections

At first, you may have to overcome inner objections, to outshout the self-esteem damaging thoughts that hamper your progress.

.

"I can't write" is common one. Of course you can! You can have a conversation, right? You have a pretty good command of the language, enough to tell a story in a few lines, can't you? There you go!

In your day to day life, you already write a lot. You compile lists, file reports, add columns, send texts, compose e-mails, write thank you notes and birthday cards, jot reminder notes, dictate business letters, applications, and letters of complaint, fill out endless forms, do homework, tweet, comment on book reviews, order products, leave To Do lists, maybe even keep a journal or write love poetry.

At first, thirty minutes may seem overwhelming, as if you couldn't possibly write anything for that long. Do it anyway! Before you know it, the words will flow, falling over themselves in their haste to get on paper.

 You may do best if you link writing to another habit you already have ingrained, such as brushing your teeth. If you decide you cannot brush your furry-feeling teeth until you write a bit, you'll find yourself reaching for a pen and paper.

Of course you are busy; we're *all* very busy. But face it---in the minutes you outright waste in a day, you could tell your story. YOUR story, from your unique perspective, in a way that only you can tell it. Do it now, for you cannot know what tomorrow will bring. Do it now, while the memories are fresh. Yes, you may have more free time when the kids are grown and you're retired, floating about on your white yacht...but that day may never come. Plus, by then, the experiences will be distant, and the memories fuzzy. Now is best!

Set a timer, and buckle down, making each writing minute precious. Just begin! You're better off actively writing than entertaining long periods of thought---

you'll soon find ideas flowing, once pen touches paper!

You may worry that you cannot think of anything to write. Once you get started, this will not be a problem, I assure you! Use the many questions in this book to jump-start your thought process. Start as though it was a fill-in-the-blank exercise, then see it build. Before you know it, your main problem will be trying to write fast enough, to capture the flood of thoughts and insights and memories that will surface!

Another common hesitation is "What will other people think?" Don't allow yourself to get hung up in other's opinions, viewpoints, or value judgments. YOUR story will be written from _your_ perspective. This is YOUR story, not theirs. They should go write their own. If you hear any objections, tell them so.

"I don't have anything important to say" can be a stumbling block. I can tell you with vehemence that you are wrong. Flat out wrong! It's best to get past that right now. Your life is worth living, and your experiences can be learned from, no matter who you are. On Life's journey, each of us learns, changes, sees, overcomes, triumphs, struggles, excels, falls down, and soars. On the way, the tales that result can be magic!

Your stories can be amazing. They can be soaring sagas of wondrous places and intriguing people, with profound insights you've garnered throughout your life. They can also be mundane, giving a brief glimpse into a time and place that is right here and right now. You may worry that you cannot think of anything to write. Once you get started, this will not be a problem, I assure you! Use the many questions in this book to jump-start your thought process. Start as though it was a fill-in-the-blank exercise, then see it build. Before you know it, your main problem will be trying to write fast enough, to capture the flood of thoughts and insights and memories that will surface!

Of course you are not limited to thirty minutes. You may well find your mind racing with more details after the timer sounds. It's perfectly okay to write a little longer, or to come back to it later in the day, or to continue the same topic in the following day's session. You have total control here. It's YOUR story, after all!

The very process of writing can offer you the opportunity to look at your life in a way you may not have seen before. Even if your childhood wasn't totally blissful, writing about it can help you sort out your feelings, from the safe distance of age and time. No one had a perfect childhood; that is why adulthood was invented. You may even find understanding, compassion, or forgiveness. Writing can be a gift you give yourself.

What about the audience? You may be very comfortable, writing your thoughts with the goal of your posterity or family or even colleagues reading it; soon, or in years to come. Other will be horrified at the very idea of anyone reading it. It's totally up to you! You may even add a disclaimer at the beginning, if it makes you feel better. "This is MY story, as I recall it" is just fine. On the other hand, you may recognize the immediate value your memories have, and find yourself making copies to send to everyone you know!

In this book, you'll learn how to easily write a story...YOUR story. You're going to write a story, not a dry historical account. It's going to be warm and full of memories, not just a list of factual facts. As you write, it will become easier to flesh it out with good detailed descriptions. Just get started---I promise, it'll be fun!

How to Write

A few ideas to shape your project:

As you write, include ordinary details, such as gas prices, tools used in your day's activities how long is your commute, who you interact with, what tv stations you watch, news stories of the day, how you get to work, etc. As you pull thoughts out of your memories, try to include as much detail as possible, for that will make your writing more rich and full. These seemingly mundane details will bring your story to life, and be interesting in years to come.

Begin writing with the goal of *writing*, not allowing trivial matters such as proper spelling, punctuation, and penmanship to get in the way. You're not writing to impress anyone. Don't get hung up on using precise grammar and big pompous words. Write as you speak; conversational stories are the best kind to read.

Always be truthful and honest about your life story. Other people who were there may have seen the same things you did, but their experience will still be very different than yours. Try not to think "is this the way everybody else viewed what happened?" Remember, it's from your own perspective. It's not their story; it's yours.

Every experience we have has both positive and less-than-positive sides to it. As you record your life's story, be careful not to focus on only the negative aspects. It's not good for your spirit, and it's most likely not honest, either. You also don't want to be Pollyanna-ish, fluffing your thoughts into a light so unfailingly positive that it isn't anywhere near reality.

 Go ahead; write about what you feel most comfortable, and recognize you are free to go back and write more later. You may feel at ease writing about major mistakes you have made, hopefully with a note about having learned something of value, or you may choose to focus on less serious topics.

As you write, you'll find the length of each segment will vary considerably. Some of your writing will be fairly brief and humorous; some longer and more serious. Sometimes you will find yourself explaining a great insight at the end of a story about what you learned, sometimes not.

How Not To Write

Many, many people have begun to record their personal history, and quit. You are going to do better!

By far the main roadblock is the self-imposed stress of trying to wrangle memories into a neat and proper chronology. Let me save you the agony....memories will surface as they please, not by any calendar's dictates. Write! Write your memories as they arise. Trying to remember details exactly in the order in which they occurred will only frustrate you, as it has so many others before you. The important thing is to tell your story!

Be careful not to critique as you write---let it flow! I advise against reading over that which you have previously written, while you're in the writing process. Inevitably, your critical mind will want to edit, or even change entire paragraphs---you might even take the dire step of throwing out whole sections, just because they don't strike your fancy when you read over them! Avoid this self-criticism, even it means you have to resort to extreme measures.

I personally clip previous pages with a paperclip. It's just enough to prevent mindless scanning. If you decide later on to publish your epic story, there will be plenty of time for editing and proofreading. If you are one of those super-organized personalities, feel free to go back and arrange your stories by age or year or even geography----*but let the story be told first.*

If you find memories surfacing faster than you can write them down, go ahead and jot a note to yourself. If you note "the day the canoe sank" or "Aunt Jelly's porcelain doll" on a bit of nearby paper, that memory will resurface when you get back to it. Capture as much as you can; don't be afraid that by writing one, you'll lose the other. The mind is a remarkable place, and nothing that goes in is ever permanently lost.

If you find yourself considering an action attached to your story, jot a note to remind yourself to do something. *Later!* Writing a thank you note to the teacher you remembered as you write your story is a fine a thing to do! But don't let it interfere with your writing. Write the thank you note at a later time.

Track down that old family recipe, by all means, just not during the designated writing period. The timer is ticking!

Tools and Places to Write

You'll be more successful if you find a comfortable place and tools with which to write.

Where should you write? Some people can write just about anywhere, perfectly happy with a half-chewed pencil, a 3 X 5 card and a knee on which to balance it. Others will find the same quiet, well-lighted place with a soft bound book gets the creativity flowing. Are you most comfortable at a desk, propped up by pillows, curled up in a window seat, sprawled on a floor? Go ahead and experiment!

You can write with any method you feel most comfortable with; any paper from a note card in your pocket to a poster board to a spiral bound notebook to a wad of notebook paper to a leather bound blank book will be fine, *so long as it's comfortable for you.* Choose something that will draw you to it, because this project is supposed to feel good, not be One More Chore To Do.

If you think you'll be writing mostly on the go, choose a book of some soft with a cover, that will not be damaged as it's in and out of your bag or pocket. If you plan to write at a desk, maybe a spiral bound book will can lay flat is ideal. You may find a fancy leather-bound blank book appeals to you, or a notebook with an appealing cover.

 Choose paper that is pleasurable to you. You may find plain white paper daunting. Fine---go with colors, or bordered paper, or hand crafted paper with warm textures. The goal here is comfort, and choosing something that feels good to you will enable you to write your story easily. Obviously, you should choose something of lasting quality, but if you want to start with a 3X 5 card, go for it.

If you choose to write by hand, a proper writing tool is essential. You may choose anything permanent ---not a smudgable pencil, no invisible ink. Avoid ink that will bleed through the paper. Choose a pen or marker that feels good in your hand, and one that flows smoothly. If you are frustrated with blips and blops and dragging the tool across the pages, you won't enjoy the writing itself. Try several pens until you find one that writes easily and does not distract from your creative thoughts. You might prefer a felt tip pen, or a quality ball point, or a smooth calligraphy pen. Which color ink makes you happy? Go ahead and change color, depending on the day and the topic and your mood!

On the other hand, you may find your stories flow better on a computer screen. That's certainly fine. Choose a word processor program that you feel at ease with, and a font that is clear to read and feels good to you. Be sure to back up your file frequently! and print pages out periodically; a hardcopy is essential.

You can even use a voice recorder, if that suits you better. You may find it easiest to simply talk, to relate your memories as they surface. Of course, it's best to transcribe them onto something more permanent (a paper form) later, but there's plenty of time for that. You may end up paying someone to type it up for you, if you choose. Lots of options!

When to Write?

Be aware of any distractions, and set them aside.
They will wait. Things always do.

Any successful endeavor requires a bit of discipline. This autobiography, too; although it's not a chore at all. Once you get started, the writing will become easier and more enjoyable. You'll find yourself thinking about your memories in between writing sessions; it can be addictive! It's your story---don't self-correct or think about what-will They-think. *Tell **your** story!*

I strongly recommend setting aside a specific place and time in which to write, with the tools you need at hand, whether they be a laptop or colorful felt pens. We are creatures of habit. It won't be long at all before your mind agrees that writing is a new habit. The very act of settling yourself in Writing Mode will cause your body to calm, and your ideas to begin flooding to the surface. All you have to do at that point is get them on paper!

Set aside thirty minutes a day, even if it requires you to get up early or turn off the TV at night. It might help you focus if you know the timer is set for a brief 30 minutes, just half an hour. Tell yourself that you are simply going to write, as fast and as steadily as possible, then stop. Don't allow random thoughts to crowd your flow of writing! This is dedicated writing time, not a time to daydream. Knowing you can stop the moment the timer goes off ---or at the end of that sentence—will help you push aside the inevitable thoughts of "I need to be doing that other thing..." Writing is valuable in and of itself—this is not time wasted!

Choosing a consistent time may be best for you. You may find writing in your pajamas in the early dawn is a great boost to your day. It may be you'd rather eat a hand-held lunch, and write as you chomp your apple. Perhaps your best time is late at night, when the day's events are past and you are safe and warm at home. You may find you write better in snippets of time, such as waiting for a bus, or for your child's practice to end, or for that meeting to begin. Carry your writing materials with you if you find you'll be stuck waiting somewhere during a day. The goal is consistency, *30 minutes a day,* in whatever form works best for you. I strongly suggest setting a timer to mark off your story-writing sessions, just at first, until it becomes ingrained.

Writing Perspective

You may write from whatever perspective feels best to you, and even change tense as desired.

First Person is easiest, as in *"I remember my Aunt Lucy's house. She lived next door to us. I thought love smelled like cinnamon, because Aunt Lucy's kitchen always had a strong cinnamon odor, no matter what she was cooking. Aunt Lucy was Dad's younger sister, and I knew she loved me. I could count on her to play with me, and give me a cookie from her house-shaped glass cookie jar, too. I wish I had the recipe for the applesauce cookies she made."*

Perhaps some parts are better written as if you were not there, just observing the scene, writing words you have heard others say, such as their emotions upon meeting the newborn who was you.

"Mom told me about the day they brought me home from the hospital. My nine year old brother had asked

for a baby brother, not a sister, and my parents worried he might not like me. Mom said he fell in love with me instantly. The next day after school, he brought his friends home to show me off. Mom said she smiled, looking at the grubby little boys surrounding my bassinette, whispering, for once, each offering a rattle or small plaything to the little baby, silently admiring little me."

You can even write in Third Person, if it feels comfortable to you.

"Jessie's favorite blanket was a gift from her Aunt Kate on her second birthday. It was soft and red. By the time Jessie had carried it everywhere she went for a few years, the blanket was faded and worn out. It was so threadbare that it eventually got a hole in the center. Jessie tearfully asked her mother to fix it. Jessie watched anxiously as her mother cut the old blanket right down the middle, and sewed the sturdier sides into a center seam, leaving the thinner parts as a hem. Even then, Jessie knew her mother loved her, because any other mother would have lectured her about how a big girl of almost five years old didn't need to drag around an old blanket. Instead, Jessie's mother sat down and fixed it right away, knowing Jessie needed it ---without a hole—to sleep with that night."

Be Liberal With Details

You're writing a story, not a dry government report. Make it come alive!

As you ponder each day's question, remember that it's not a fill-in-the-blank test. Don't use one-word answers, unless you need to jot a note for when you come back to that particular question at a later time.

See the difference?

Question: *have you seen changes in the political climate since your childhood?*

Answer: *Yes, I have seen some.*

Answer: *I was a young teenager during the Viet Nam war, and it seemed that the whole United States was on edge. The security I felt as a young child faded,* *although I think my Mom did her best to shield us kids from news of the war. Many of my older sister's school friends served in the military. I saw they were not respected when they came home. Where were the parades that had welcomed home soldiers in previous conflicts? I recalled Grandma telling of how proud she was to have her sons both serve in the Great War, as she called it. That contrasted with overhearing Mom fervently praying that the Viet Nam war would be over before her boys would be old enough for the draft. I noticed the adults around me, especially my father, seemed disgusted with the way the media covered the news. He'd sit in the blue easy chair every night before dinner with his newspaper, and snort as he read parts of articles aloud. I think that is when the country began to lose faith in the government, to think that it was Us and Them. It seems to me that, before then, citizens trusted their elected leaders. Since then, I've seen Watergate, and its impact on the country, and because of that I think..."*

Ask yourself questions to jog your memory: where was it? What details especially stand out (odors, sounds, fabrics, scenery, colors, background items, etc)? Who all was present? What were the circumstances? What caused this memory to surface just now? Can you recall how you felt? Do any bits of conversation come to mind? Include why? how? when? where? who was there? and then what? Think of the way your favorite novels are written, with enough details to let the reader imagine the site. It takes only a few words to bring a scene or person to life.

Use whole names, and places, not just "Tommy" or "the cabin at the lake." Tell your relationship with Tommy---is he a brother, uncle, neighbor? Your sister's boyfriend? Is he your age, younger, or older? Did you like him, fear him, know him well? Who owned the cabin? Could you find it on a map, or at least give a nearby town? Did you spend every summer there, or was it a one-time vacation with a childhood friend's family? Can you describe it? _You_ know what you are talking about; generations to come won't have a clue. You don't have to use complete names every single time you refer to a person or place, but do it at least once.

"As we sung on the rope swing, Joe walked up."

"As my brother, Lew, and I swung out over Franklin Lake on the rope swing tied to the big oak, old Joe Thom walked up. Joe owned the tree and the rope, and he had warned us not to play on it. We knew we were in big trouble."

See the difference?

How to Write, Using Prompts

*The next section is the **questions and prompts** that will get your thoughts flowing.*

Consider them as jumping-off points. You're not bound to write about each one, or in the order they are written here. Use them to get your story started. Before long, you may very well find your ideas start to flow without the prompts. Go for it—it's *your* story!

You will likely come upon a question or a prompt that just doesn't fit your life. Maybe you're not married, have no career, never had a vacation, don't wish to remember your abusive Uncle Ted. It's okay to skip over it, so long as you *keep writing!* If a story or memory is too uncomfortable to write at this time, just move on past it.

Go ahead and write out-of-order, not following the prompts as they are written, making your own way. No one is judging you here; you're doing this for YOU.

Look at the questions/prompts, and expand on them.
A one-word response isn't the goal! Ponder them; roll
them around in your mind. Let your mind roll back in
time, seeing the scene in your mind's eye as if you are
reliving it. Adding small details will round out your
story, plus you'll have the additional benefit of
revisiting the memory as it plays out in your mind's
eye.

As you face each writing session's question, see if you
are best served by dividing the story by time. For
instance, your ten-year-old Self had a world view that
your teen Self did not value, and as an adult, your
whole perspective may be very different yet again.
Are you most at ease writing in each time period?
Decide if you are comfortable thinking in terms of
childhood, youth, current or past, present,
future...You should do what feels best, recognizing it'll
change as you tell your story.

The prompts are in an order that seems reasonable to
me, but may not suit you at all. You may prefer to
write straight through about one section, or jump
around, as the mood strikes. If you are happier writing

absolutely everything you recall about your teen years, go ahead and skim through, stopping at the questions regarding that season of your life, then move on.

You will notice that some of the prompts seem repeated, or perhaps worded in a slightly different way. That's intentional. As you look at them, memories will rise to the surface, and you will find yourself thinking about the same circumstances in different ways. That's a great way to let your story flow, recording details each time. The suggestions along with the questions are just to rattle memories loose; don't be limited by them.

Let's get started! Choose a prompt, set your timer, and jump right in.

Who Am I?

In all the billions of people who have ever taken their place on Earth, there is only one <u>you</u>, with your experiences. Start at the beginning.

What is your full and complete name? How was your name chosen? By whom? Are you aware of any stories surrounding it?

Do you like your name? Does it seem to "fit" you? Do you have a nickname?

You know how to politely introduce others, telling something interesting and positive about them. How would you introduce yourself?

All of us have turning points, major events that shape our future path. What milestones can you identify in your life?

How did your family come to be living where you were born? Did they immigrate recently, or have they there for generations?

Can you sketch a simple timeline of your life? It seems simple, but putting milestones on paper can be illuminating!

Do you speak a foreign language? How did you learn it? Has it been useful?

A lifelong friend is a rare gift. Who do you count as true friends? Have you kept in touch with any of your childhood friends?

Astronaut, ballerina? What did you "want to be when you grow up"? Has it changed?

What do you wish people knew about you? Are you secretly shy? That you feel much younger than the face in your mirror? That keeping your opinions to yourself seems polite, but causes stomach pain?

Do people say you have a regional accent? Are they right? What influenced it?

What was your unspoken childhood role in the family? Peacemaker, baby, leader, little adult?

We all have some vanity. What physical traits are your best?

Often we cannot see our own talents, but they are obvious to others. What compliments stand out in your mind? Has anyone verbally appreciated something you have done for them or others?

Is there something you'd change about your physical self if you could do so? Do you long to be taller, slimmer, have red curly hair, do you desire broader shoulders, or would you just like to be free from allergies and chronic pain?

Describe yourself to a distant person you've not met yet, well enough for them to spot you on sight.

What have you discovered about yourself recently?

Would you consider yourself to be a creative person? How so? In what areas?

When you look up in the vast empty sky, what do you feel?

Tell about a kindness you received or witnessed that changed the way you look at life.

If you are a younger sibling, what stories do you know about how they welcomed you? Open arms and joyful, disdain, apathy?

Childhood

We have to rely on the memory of others before our own is fully formed. Sometimes the stories we have heard others tell of people and events color the way we think of those people or events, later on in life.

What is your very earliest memory? How old were you at the time?

What stories about your early childhood do you remember hearing others tell?

Children often have a security object. What was yours? Did it have a name? Do you still have it, discreetly tucked away?

Did you have an allowance when you were a child? Was it earned or given?

What did you spend your childhood funds on? What did you save up for? Were you the best customer of that old-fashioned candy store around the corner, or did you save up to buy your own pony at age nine?

What are your birthday memories from childhood? Did you have birthday parties, or special treats?

Which birthday stands out most in your memory?

What did you like to do outdoors when you were a child?

Did you have a favorite plaything? Where is it now?

Tell about your childhood experience with grown-up parties. Were you allowed to attend, even briefly, did you peek through the banisters, hoping to remain unseen, or were you sent to bed early?

What were your favorite family activities as a child? Have you carried any of them into adulthood?

How did your family work together, play together, worship together, celebrate together?

Would you say you were a happy child?

As a child, did you have a beloved pet? How old were you, where did it come from, what did you enjoy about it? Describe it, and add others' comments if you recall them.

Who was your favorite adult? What drew you to them?

How would you describe yourself as a child?

Tell about any childhood moves to a new neighborhood or city. How did it change you?

What organized groups did you belong to as a child, (Scouts, 4-H, church groups, and so on)? Who do you remember being with you? In what ways was it beneficial?

Who did you look up to as a child? Was there someone you aspired to be like?

Tell about an odd gift you were given as a child. Green Stamps? a duckling? the deed to a property? What made it seem odd to you? Was it the wrong size, style, age?

Describe your bedroom when you were a child. Did it contain treasures?

Who came to visit your childhood home? Was your home a place where neighbors gathered, did your parents host family dinners, was it a place where the kids' friends preferred to hang out?

Who loved you when you were little? How did you know?

Most children feel safest at home. Can you write about the earliest times you spent the night away from home? Where were you, with whom, why? How did you feel?

What item from your childhood do you still love?

Parental expectations have a huge influence on a child! What were some of your parent's expectations? Obedience, free thinking, discipline, athleticism, following in their career path?

What were your childhood toys? What became of them? Do you still have any of them?

What are some childhood memories regarding weekends? Did your family stay home to work and worship, go skiing every weekend, were weekends like every other day?

Was your family the go-and-do kind, or more stay-at-home?

What do you wish your parents had taught you better? Did you wish they taught you to wash dishes, or about prejudice, or to ride a horse?

How did you view the world as a child? Safe and secure, unstable and unpredictable? Why?

Who did you trust as a child?

The way we see our parents interact literally changes the way we love others later in life. How did your parents show love to one another?

How did you know your parents loved you? How did they show it?

Who was your main caregiver? Were you at home with mommy, at daycare, with a variety of babysitters?

What are your very earliest memories? Think back--- there are surely very early snippets of times and places.

Did your childhood family go on vacations? Where? What stands out in your mind?

Have you tried going back to your special childhood places? Were they as you remembered?

What do you remember about your early school years? Did your kindergarten class have a sandbox, built right into the classroom floor? Was there a reading room, a playground, strict discipline?

What scared you as a child? Does it still concern you?

What kind of a child were you? Quiet, rowdy, a bully, a loner, diligent, playful, happy, studious, reckless, obedient, outgoing, defiant, precocious? Describe that you-child, as if you'd just met.

Do you recall a time you first slept outdoors? What stands out in your mind about it?

Tell about a promise made to you in your childhood that was kept.

Can you think of any broken promises? How did they impact you at the time? Do they still matter to you?

What were your parent's roles in your childhood family? Did Dad do the yard work, and Mom the cooking, or was your family less traditional?

Who taught you to read? Do you remember favorite books?

Tell about childhood celebrations. Most families acknowledge birthdays; what other days call for a celebration?

What were your childhood interests or hobbies? Rockets, reading, dolls, painting?

Were you involved with sports as a young child?

Who did you play with when you were a child? Tell about your friends.

What were some of your childhood responsibilities?

What was your first experience with people who were different than you? How did it change your young perspective?

Most children have a favorite play-place, such as a tree house, under the bush in the back yard, behind the couch, or on the porch. Where was yours? Describe it.

Tell about your early school years. What do you remember about your classroom? Teacher? Friends? Take a few writing blocks to expand on this.

Did your family have religious traditions?

Who taught you to ride a bike?

What do you recall other significant adults teaching you?

Youth and Teen Years

Teen years are the time when you grow from a child, dependent on parents and adults to a more free-standing individual, full of hopes and promise.

Who were your closest friends as a teen?

Did your childhood friends carry over into your youth?

When you were a teen, what were your favorite things to do?

What was your first paid job? Lawn mowing, babysitting, delivering newspapers? Tell about it.

Who was your favorite teacher, and why were they special to you? Did their influence cause any course corrections in your life?

Times change, and fashion along with it. What kinds of clothing did you usually wear to school? Was there a dress code?

What type of music was important to you? Did you have a favorite group/singer/ artist?

When you were a teen, what made you feel confident?

As you watched the adults in your life, how did that color your view on adult roles? Did you follow their footsteps, or determine to make your own way?

Who was your best advocate, the one person who always believed in you?

What was your favorite outfit as a teen? How did it make you feel? Confident, pretty, invincible, rebellious?

As a young person, what difficulties did you face? Family upheaval, school problems, loss of a close friend, perhaps?

Who did you know you could always count on?

Did you have extended family gatherings when you were younger? Describe them. Where, who was there, what did everyone do, what was the atmosphere like?

What was your relationship like with your siblings as a teen? Did it seem different than in younger years?

What were your interests or hobbies in your youth?

What or who inspired you as a youth? Athletes, religious leaders, older family members, a teacher?

When you were a teen, what were your ambitions and goals? College, making the team, romance?

What groups were you a part of? Teams, troops, troupes?

What kind of a teen were you? Confident, fearful, outgoing, reserved, studious, sports-obsessed, popular, reliable, obstinate, hard working?

Who taught you to drive? Do you recall your feelings at that time?

Do you remember any fads during your youth? Goldfish swallowing, leg warmers, disco dancing, tie dye shirts?

When did you first vote? Can you recall where and for whom you voted? How did you feel?

Trauma can be cumulative. Did you develop any new fears as a teen? Tell the story.

What were your family responsibilities as a teenager? Did you do most of the cooking, help care for younger children, mow the lawn, or were you told that only your studies mattered?

What was one thing you hoped to do when you were grown up and on your own?

Who influenced you as a teen? Why do they stay in your memory?

Tell about your personal space as a teen. Did you have your own room, an off-limits box, a corner of the garage that was all your own?

What place did religion and spirituality have in your youth?

What did you cherish?

Who was your most challenging teacher in school? What made that so?

What skills did you notice you possessed in your teens? Music, mechanics, dance, performing arts?

What was worth any effort in your teen years? A dream, academics, holding your family together, making the team, perhaps?

Who was the oldest person you can remember in your family when you were growing up? How did you feel about them? What do you remember about them?

What were some of your most prized possessions?

Adulthood

Of course, much of who we are as adults is shaped by earlier years, but adults have more freedom to choose their paths.

Now that you have the wisdom of years, what do you genuinely like about yourself?

What kind of an adult are you? Would you call yourself calm, organized, flighty, hardworking, religious, haphazard, loving, protective, angry, reliable?

What do you prefer to wear as an adult? Can you describe your personal style? Do you enjoy dressing up, or is a tee shirt and shorts pretty much your uniform?

What part has art played in your life? Have you taken any formal classes?

What are you confident in now?

As an adult, what's one thing you'd like to change about yourself? Is it possible? Is it time to think about a plan?

Not including your home, where do you feel most 'at home'?

What are your free-time interests or hobbies? Do any of them carry over from your youth?

Do you have a Go To outfit, that makes you feel confident? A special sweater, a favorite tie, neon underwear?

What difficult situations have you faced? Write about the first one that comes to mind; there's a reason that memory surfaced.

What do you enjoy doing with friends?

We're all uneasy at times. What makes you feel secure now?

What music is important to you? Does classical music always calm you? Do you turn to jazz for motivation?

What part do sports play in your life? Participant, spectator, fan, no interest?

What do you wish your parents had taught you?

Quick---write all the reasons you'd like to own a working magic wand. What do you long to change?

What brings you outright, pure joy?

What is the most memorable gift you ever received? Who gave it to you? What does it mean to you?

How do you respond to injustice?

What is your role in your home? Protector, listening ear, bread-winner, nurturer, fix-it person, the one who plays with children?

What do you expect from yourself?

Do you tend to make friends easily? Tell about a close friend, either a childhood or current one.

What are your political views, currently?

Do you live in a place with changing seasons? How do you think that affects your mood?

What are your relationships with your siblings like as an adult? How have they changed over the years? Do you think childhood roles still surface?

Have you had any mentors in your career? What have you learned from them?

How have you been a mentor to others?

What was your paid job through most of your working life? What have you learned from it? Do you find it worthwhile?

Who do you trust, no matter what?

A reset button would be handy. If you long for a "do-over" in your life, what would it be?

What accomplishment do you feel really good about?

What do you cherish in your life?

What event or circumstance made you realize "I'm an adult now"?

What have you enjoyed about each season of your life? Do you long to be young again, or are you grateful you'll never have to go through _that_ again?

What is an unfulfilled dream?

When do you feel a sense of satisfaction?

Why do you live where you currently call home? Adults get to choose, and it's a big wide world.

What is one of the most surprising things that has happened to you?

What is of most value to you? Why?

What type or genre of book do you enjoy reading? How have your tastes changed over the years?

Write about a simple kindness you offered recently.
How did it feel?

What new hobby would you like to take up, if you
could? Would you golf, or dance, or throw pottery?

What do you wish for?

Day to Day Life

Yes, your day to day life seems pretty routine to you, but will be endlessly fascinating to generations to come! Include mundane things such as prices, routes, tools used, etc.

What part does the media play in your life? Are you constantly connected, or happiest "unplugged"? Would you call yourself a news junkie?

What do you enjoy during leisure times? Tv, hobby, sports, cloud-gazing?

What do you think about when you don't have to think about anything?

If someone came to you and offered to do something for you, to make your life easier, what would you tell them?

Do you consider yourself a homebody, or do you love entertaining and socializing?

What do you see as your current responsibilities? How have they changed over the years? How do you feel about them?

What is your financial outlook? Are you more of a saver, or a spender? What contributes to that attitude?

Do you prefer background sounds, such as music, or silence?

Perspective changes over the years. What are some current prices for items you routinely purchase?

Everyone talks to themselves, whether they admit it or not! What do you talk about?

Where are you most at ease?

Can you write your schedule for a typical day? It'll be interesting to read down the road.

Marriage and Romance

Adult relationships both show who we are, and shape who we are.

Tell about your first love. Who was it, how old were you, how did you 'know'?

If you're married, what did you look for in a future spouse?

What attracted you to your spouse? Looks, talents, the way he treated his mother, the way she drew people to her?

Where did you meet your spouse? Blind date, college class, aunt's house?

How old were you when you married? How did this influence you? Would you advise others to marry younger, or wait considerably longer?

Tell about meeting your future in laws. Did you feel accepted? Did they like you? What as your first impression?

Weddings can be a challenge! Tell about planning yours. Did other people help, or "help?"

 What do you recall about your wedding day? Who was there? What were your dominant emotions? Describe clothes, weather, unplanned adventures, etc. Take as much time as you need.

What would you have liked to have done differently? Eloped, had a bigger celebration, saved the money spent on the lavish reception to buy a house?

What has been your hardest adjustment in marriage?

What types of things do you find most romantic?
Love notes, fancy dinner, roses, help washing the car?

What do you wish you could tell your spouse?

Which stage of your relationship has been the most difficult?

What are some mutual dreams?

Which stage of your relationship has been the most enjoyable?

Do you feel your spouse supports you? (it's not about money!)

How could you be a better partner?

What draws you closer to one another?

What adventures have you enjoyed with your spouse?

What lies ahead?

Homes

Every home is different, with its own atmosphere, décor, and occupants. How have your residences influenced you?

Can you list all the places where you have lived? Can you recall addresses, too?

Describe your home now. How did you come to be living there?

What would you like to change about it? Who makes those decisions?

If your house caught fire, what items would you grab as you fled? Photos, computer, the cat?

What do you recall about your childhood home?

What kind of a home have you secretly dreamed of living in? Elegant tree house, a yurt, a glass house on your own private island, a centuries-old castle, perhaps?

Describe the neighborhood you lived in as a child. Was it a big city, small town, or a farm? Do you think it impacted your outlook on life?

In what room at your home are you most at ease? What do you enjoy best about it?

Describe your present home. Who lives there? What do you like about it? What would you like to change?

Travel and Socializing

It's a big wide world out there!

Everyone is different. Do you enjoy being around people, or are you content in your own space?

What is your outlook on travel? Are you happiest at home, or do you have wanderlust?

Where have you traveled? States, countries? Cities, parks, the seashore?

Are you happiest returning to the same place again and again, or exploring new destinations?

What has been your best vacation as an adult?

What was your first experience with foreign food like? Do you remember what, where, with whom?

Where would your dream vacation take you? What appeals to you about that dream?

What is the most beautiful place you have ever visited? What was it like? Would you like to return?

If you could visit a new city for just one day, where would you head first? Museum, art gallery, parks, restaurant, trails, shopping center? Is this typical of your traveling style?

What are your experiences with performance art? Do you love opera, seek out community theaters, enjoy concerts?

What has been your greatest adventure, so far?

What adventure do you dream of?

Is traveling important to you? Do you wish to see the world, or are you more of a homebody?

Where do you dream of traveling? Are your dreams possible?

When guests come to visit from out of town, what do you show them? Do you book a show, take them hiking, go shopping, visit nearby historic places?

What is the most interesting vehicle you've ever employed? Hot air balloon, spaceship, elephant? Tell the story.

Silence is rare sometimes! Where was the quietest place you've experienced? How did you feel there?

Sometimes, there really is no place like home. Tell about an interesting place you discovered, not far from home.

What is your favorite means of travel? Airplane, boat, hiking boots, camelback?

How do you act like a tourist in your own hometown? Do you seek new restaurants, museums, hiking trails, theatres?

Family Life

One of the joys of life is in having your own family, and there is probably no greater influence on society.

Do you have children? Tell about their beginnings; how you found out they were coming, your emotions surrounding that time. You'd better take more than one writing session for this!

What do you remember most clearly about your children's births? Who was in attendance? How did you feel? Was it a calm time, or an emergency situation?

How were your children's names chosen? Did others have any say in the matter? Are they family names, names from the Top Ten list, made-up ones? Do they have special meaning to you?

Tell about each of your children. In what ways are they similar to, and different than, one another?

When did you first see your child as a person in his or her own right, instead of an extension of yourself?

What do you do really well in regards to your children? Are you a good listener, can you calm a child easily, did you teach them to budget their money?

If your children had known you as a child or teen, what would they have thought about that younger you? Would you two have been friends?

Raising children is hard work, although very rewarding. What do you count as your biggest challenges in raising your children?

If you had it to do all over again, knowing what you know now, would you change the way you raised your family? How?

What does your family do for pure fun? games, sports, day trips, cooking together?

What do you think you have learned from parenting?

How would you describe your parenting style? Laid back, intense, lenient, strict, inconsistent, strong?

One of the drawbacks of aging is that once you acquire skills and insights, no one seems to want them. What would be your best advice to young parents?

What do you wish you had known as a young parent?

What do you wish someone had told you ahead of time? Would it have changed things?

Write about some traditions unique to your family. Do you celebrate the first day of summer, watch meteor showers in the back yard, have an annual bike hike?

What have you learned from your children?

What are some life skills you taught your children as they were growing up?

Tell about your family's childhood traditions. Holidays, back yard campouts, encounters with The Tooth Fairy?

Who gave you parenting advice when your children were young?

What do you admire or even envy about your children?

What do you and your children enjoy about one another now? Do you share interests, are you able to learn new things together, do you enjoy just being together?

What quirks does your family have? Write about something you're pretty sure other families just don't do.

What is something you think every child should know? That they are valued, manners, obedience, flexibility, budgeting?

What is something your children would be shocked to know about you? Did you attend a Southern Charm School, play in a band, hike across Asia?

What do you wish you could change in your family?

Extended Family

Grandparents, aunts, uncles, even baby cousins all have an impact on us, giving us the anchors we crave and the freedom to step aside as well.

Who are your siblings? Where do they –and you—fit in the family?

Did you ever wish you had another sibling, or a few more? Or did you long to be an only child?

Did you get along well with your siblings when you were children?

Do you get along well with your siblings now?

If you have a younger sibling, what do you remember about the circumstances of that birth?

How were holidays celebrated in your home growing up? Did extended family members and friends attend, or was it low-key?

Are you celebrating differently now?

What were the opinions of children by older family members? Seen but not heard? Valued, indulged, or set at the dreaded Children's Table?

What causes pride when you think about those who came before you? Were they patriots, heroes, civil servants, good parents?

Do you know where your strongest personal convictions originated? Is your mother known for organization, your father for his work ethic, your grandfather for his musical talent?

Who did you feel closest to, growing up?

How do you remember your grandparents? Expand on the ones you remember, giving time to each. Take more than one writing session; they were whole people

What was important to your parents? Values, skills, dedication, sports?

Write about your mother.

Tell about your father.

How would you classify your family's socioeconomic level? Just getting by, middle class, way above most folks? Can you see how this influenced you, and continues to do so?

What do you wish you knew about your ancestors?

What are the roles you and your siblings took on in your family of origin? Were you the responsible one, the peacemaker, the baby? Do you still maintain those roles today?

Did you have extended family members, such as aunts, uncles, grandparents, living near you as you grew up? Tell about them.

Who were some of the oldest family members you can recall? What do you know about them?

How would you describe your parents' relationship? Do you wonder if that has any basis in reality? Would they see it the same way, do you think?

What roles did you observe in the adults in your family? How did they color your own roles?

What do you respect about previous generations? Was life easier, or more difficult then? In what ways?

Did you have extended family gatherings when you were younger? Describe them. Where, who was there, what did everyone do, what was the atmosphere like?

What have you learned from extended family members?

Who would you say is the "anchor" in your extended family?

Which extended family members influenced you the most?

Write a story that is part of family lore, one that is told over and over.

Other People

Family is not the only influence---who else has touched your life?

Which of your neighbors has had the most influence in your life, for good or ill? Did the woman down the street teach you to be confident, or that man help you build your garage, or did you learn that being the meanest grouch on the block is not the way to be happy?

Have you ever received a letter or note that influenced your life? Write about it, and what changed because of it.

If you were to take time to write a letter to someone who influenced your life, who would it be? What did they do?

Detail a small yet valued kindness, and how it made you feel. Was it a co-worker who listened, a classmate who stood up for you, a stranger who held traffic so you could back the car out?

Have you met any "celebrities" or famous people? Did you sneak backstage at a Beatles concert? introduce a famous speaker? share an elevator with a celeb? Describe what happened, and how you felt at the time.

Can you relate a conversation that sticks with you?

Have you experienced any form of culture shock in your life?   Where was it, and how did it affect your outlook?

What do you wish had been left unsaid?

Good deeds are important! Can you remember a recent good deed done for you?   What have you done for someone else? How did it feel?

Who has challenged you? How did the experience change you?

What kinds of people interest you?

Dreams, Hopes, and Aspirations

Regardless of how you actually live your life, all of us have dreams and wishes of ways to make it better.

What is one area in your life you wish you could improve? What's stopping you?

What would you most like to be known for?

What is the greatest life lesson you have learned?

What is a life skill you wish you had? Do you wish you could sew, manage money better, adapt to new situations more easily?

Would you say you trust easily? Why or why not?

Tell about an Ah-Ha! moment. What did you learn?

What do you wish was different?

What is one thing you regret not teaching your children? Is it too late?

Would you rather have a magic wand or a crystal ball? Would you rather know what lies ahead, or fix things you already see?

What brings you peace?

What amazed you, even now?

What is missing in your life?

What is one thing that would make you feel better, right now? Taking off your shoes, eating a snack, watching fireflies?

What is your best asset?

What is one thing you wish others could see in you?

If untold wealth suddenly befell you, what would you do first? Who would you tell first?

Do you recall any words of wisdom in your life; a time when someone said something that really made a difference to you?

Who understands you better than anyone else in the world?

What are some good things you see in the world around you?

What traits would you like to be known for? Strength, compassion, joyfulness, efficiency?

What do you value? Is it a tangible item, a trait, a belief system?

How do you counter everyday stress? Music, a walk, a snack, talking it out?

Every life has a few pivot points, when the course of a lifetime turns in a completely different direction. What comes to mind?

What is lacking in your life currently, the one thing you long for? Is it love, acceptance, a listening ear, diamond ropes? What would be different if this desire was met?

What is one of your strongest character traits? Are you relentlessly honest? a hard worker? do you never quit? Tell about a time you brought it to the forefront.

What are some of your strongest personal convictions and values? Do you know what formed them?

Tell about a place that warms your heart.

In a crisis, how do you cope? Are you the strong one, the one who runs for aid, the one who is usually frozen in fear?

When you long for life to just slow down, what aspects do you look at first?

What are your current political leanings? How have they changed over the years?

If you could turn back time, which day would you relive? Why?

Who hurt your feelings? Looking back, do you see things any differently?

What adventures are yet to come?

Experiences

Every person's experiences are different. How have yours determined your path?

What are some of your off-the-wall talents? Can you ride a unicycle, decorate wedding cakes, whistle through a straw?

Tell about an unexpected windfall and its impact on your life.

What has changed most in your lifetime?

Have you experienced any catastrophes, such as earthquakes, tornadoes, house fire, floods, etc? Where were you? What was it like, and what was the aftermath? Do you think it changed the way you look at things?

Escapism is the act of mentally stepping off the world, by whatever method you choose. What works for you? Is it going to a movie, reading, artwork, traveling, staring at the stars?

How has your financial situation impacted your life? Have you been jarred by extreme poverty, or felt uneasy around great wealth or celebrity?

Have you felt out of place in various groups of people, or are you pretty much able to fit in anywhere?

The world is moving fast! What inventions have you seen during your lifetime?

What activities do you find rewarding?

There is much good in the world, and not all of it is readily explained. What miracles have you witnessed?

What inventions have made your life easier? Plastic wrap, cell phones, super glue?

What innovations have you seen in your lifetime?

Have you seen anything supernatural, such as a ghost or UFO? Tell about it.

Describe an experience with public performance. What did you do? How did you feel?

Everyone has setbacks in their lives. What was yours, and how did you bounce back from it?

Tell about a loss in your life. How did it impact you?

What unpaid efforts have brought you pleasure?

When do you recall first taking a step towards independence? Was it when you first crossed a street with no one holding your hand? when you went to summer camp? when you moved into the college dorm?

Is there an odor or aroma that can transport you back to another place in time, a scent with a strong memory attached? Does pine cleaner remind you of Grandma, or do strawberries transport you to lazy summer days at the beach?

Many people carry or possess an item of no real monetary value, yet it often has a strong memory attached. It might be a rock, or a seashell, a broken chain, or a bit of glass. Do you have one? What memory is connected with it?

Tell about a time when you were coerced into doing something or going somewhere where you did not wish to go. What was the outcome? Did it turn into a good experience after all?

What is the best sound in the world to you? How does it make you feel? A baby's laughter, coins falling, waves crashing on a rocky beach?

Food Memories

Many of our memories are centered around food. Often, just the aroma of a dish can transport our thoughts to another time.

Do you recall any food traditions in your childhood family? Did your mother always cut the sandwiches in triangles, or serve ketchup on French toast? Was ham always on the Christmas table? Did your father do the grilling?

What are your favorite recipes? Is there a memory associated with them?

What was the first food you recall cooking all by yourself? Scrambled eggs at age two, grilled cheese at age seven, ramen at college?

Which section do you look at first on a restaurant menu? Are you a virtuous salad-eater, or do you think dessert is the only reason to eat out?

Tell about your family mealtimes as a child. Who cooked them, most of the time? Did you gather to eat together, or did everyone just fill a plate and go to their room? Was conversation a big part of mealtime?

Who prepares food in your home most of the time? Do you know why?

Tell about some signature meals you recall.

What foods make you recall happy times?

Are there any un-typical food traditions in your family now? Do you serve ravioli on Thanksgiving, or always have peach jam on your omelets?

Do you have a go-to recipe? What is it? Where did you first taste it?

Who was the main person who cooked when you were younger? Did this influence you, beyond nutrition?

Can you recall any special foods made by extended family? Did your Italian grandfather make wine-infused sausage and prosciutto in the basement, did your aunts make Greek pastry? did your brother in law grill salmon with basil sauce? Tell about these memories.

Personal and Personality Traits

We all have talents. Some are very obvious, such a piano playing or organizing events effortlessly.

We also have talents no one sees. What are <u>your</u> best hidden talents? Are you a skilled bargain-hunter, can you plan a dinner for thirty in ten minutes flat, can you motivate a group easily?

Tell about your best day ever. What made it special?

How would you define your conversational style? Are you more of a listener, or do you tend to run others over? Are you able to draw people into a conversation, or do they seem invisible to you?

What are some of the best choices you've ever made? How did they impact your life?

Think about an influential book you've read. How did it change the way you think?

How do you interact with nature? Do you enjoy hiking and camping, or are you most at ease viewing nature though magazine layouts?

What makes you different from a room full of random people?

What do you enjoy doing for others?

What would you most like to be remembered for?

Finish this thought: "Someday, I'm going to ..."

Do you think the way others see you is the way you see yourself? What do others see in you that you overlook? The easiest way is to think of compliments. Do others say that you are put together, on top of things, always late...?

Do you tend to be unfailingly prompt, or running late? Do you know what set this habit?

What kind of a shopper are you? A frugal bargain hunter, a grab-it-and-go-get-just-what-you-need type, a lingering browser? Do you know what set this pattern?

What has been your greatest adventure, so far?

What adventure do you dream of?

Who do you respect? Why?

Where do you feel most safe?

What makes you laugh?

What have you always wished to visit or see?

What life-changing event do you never speak of? A crime, a miracle?

What is the most memorable gift you have ever given to someone?

Who do you aspire to be like?

What is your most comfortable time of day? Why?

When was a time you really relied on God?

When have you pushed past your "comfort zone" and done some unexpected and out of your routine? Did you sign up for a sign-language class, bring home a pet monkey, repaint the bedroom neon orange? What was the result?

What makes you happy?

What makes you feel anxious?   What keeps you up at night?

Do you see everyday skills in yourself that others lack? Are you a skilled shopper, able to make a meal out of a near-empty pantry, can you roof a house singlehandedly, are you an innate organizer, can you calm a child in mere moments?

Finish this thought: "I have always wished for..."

What is your best trait?

Tell about a character trait you wish you had. Do you long to be braver, more honest, tougher in some way?

What kind of people are you drawn to?

Is there a "category' of people you are uneasy around? Loud-mouths, those who are different than you, older people, children, the poor, the wealthy?

Would you consider yourself racist, age-ist, elitist, or any other kind of –ist?

Do you tend to act impulsively, or think things through first?

Detail a time when you felt at peace, just happy to be alive. What were the circumstances?

Would you consider yourself a leader or a follower? Can you relate a story where you took the lead?

What part does technology play in your life? Do you jump to have the newest-and-greatest? Is your email program the same one used by the pioneers crossing the plains? Is your electronic device practically surgically implanted in your hand, or do you disdain any technology invented after your high school years?

Would you consider yourself a daydreamer? What tends to be your major theme or topic?

What is guaranteed to make you smile, every time?

People often do what they do because that's what they have always done. Can you tell of a time when you stepped out of character? What happened?

What do you specifically admire in others? Do you wish you had that poise, drive, compassion, courage, ease in solving problems?

What do you count as a major accomplishment, so far?

When you feel homesick, what place comes to mind?

Describe a dream day. If you could plan a full 24 hours perfectly, what would it look like? Who would it include?

Tell about a sad time in your life.

When you dream of sudden wealth, how would you use it first?

Tell about a time when you were so happy, you could feel joy bubble up under your ribs.

Do you feel national pride? When and about what in particular?

When you look up in the vast empty sky, what do you feel?

Have you seen changes in the political climate since your childhood?

Do you have any personal traditions? Do you always watch meteor showers in August, buy daisies on Thursdays, or eat jellybeans at the movies?

What do you specifically admire in yourself? Do you consider yourself a good listener, a great cook, a fine public speaker, kind-hearted?

Would you call yourself well informed, or are you just as happy not knowing? Has age changed your opinion?

What is your decision making style?

What music can make your spirits soar, every time?

Is there a quote that sticks in your mind, surfacing as needed?

Health

*Some people just seem to be accident prone.
Others reach old age with nary a broken bone. All
impact our life.*

Write about any accidents and injuries you've had.
Did you learn anything from the experience?

How do you behave when you feel poorly? Up and at
'em anyway, or do you recline in a bathrobe with hot
soup?

What is a long-term habit that you are trying to
break?

Your body is a miracle. What is your best feature?

We all have to put on a Brave Act at times in our lives. Can you think of times when you stretched past a fear or phobia?

Have you had a health scare? Tell about it.

What is your philosophy on health?

How do you respond in an emergency? Do you calmly jump in to help, or fall apart and join in the screaming? Are you more likely to step away and call for someone else to help?

We grow stronger from overcoming obstacles. What have you overcome?

Who would most miss you after you die?

What was your first experience with death? Expand.

Beliefs and Values

Our belief system and values are set very early in life, and form the center of our character.

What is it that you would protect with your very life, if necessary?

What do you look forward to about aging?

What do you fear about growing older?

What do you value most? Your family, your home, your career, that special book?

Are you generally the first to dive in, or are you content on the sidelines?

Without putting a lot of thought into it, quickly list 25 things for which you are thankful, small and large. Freedom, family, socks?

Who do you respect? Can you say why?

What do you cherish about your country of birth?

Have you seen true courage? What did it look like to you?

Would you consider yourself competitive? What influences this?

What brings you joy? Would you say you are generally introverted or an extrovert? Does this change in different circumstances?

Do you have a regret? Is there any way to remedy it? A note, an apology, perhaps?

Where do your loyalties lie, primarily?

What Legacies Carry On?

What is a family story told that carries down through the years, like a thread across generations?

As you look back over your life from this viewpoint, what are a few things you wish you had done that you have not? Have you always longed to sky dive, run for public office, perform stand-up comedy onstage, visit every state in North America, or swim with eels?

What is some advice you've heard all your life? Who said it?

What do you want to be remembered for? Accomplishments, character, devotion, academic degrees?

What is some wisdom or advice given to you by an older person? Did you brush it off, or make it a part of you?

What words of wisdom do you recall your parents saying?

What legacy would you like to leave your children?

One of the drawbacks of aging is that by the time we accrue wisdom, it seems no one wants it. If you could share your wisdom with those following in your footsteps, what would it be?

What is the best advice you have ever given?

What do you wish you knew about your parents? Who were they before you came into their lives?

Can you relate a story about your parents?

What are your dreams for your children and grandchildren?

What do you wish your great-grandchildren would know?

What do you want for your children?

What do you want to be remembered for?

Write some advice you wish to share with future generations. These words may be the most precious words you leave to your loved ones!

Wrap It Up

It's YOUR story! No one is as qualified as you to tell it!

There may be some prompts you'd like to revisit, as you wind up your legacy. As you continue to write, what areas of your life do you feel inclined to change, just because of this process?

Looking back over what you have written can cause even more memories and dreams to surface. It's time to look over your personal story, and see what you'd like to write next. You can write your story in only 30 minutes a day, but there are many days left in your life, so don't stop now!

****

Be sure to take a minute to leave a positive review! You can even be anonymous, if you wish.

Livelihoods depend on good reviews, and I greatly appreciate yours.

Other Books By Deb Graham:

Tips From The Cruise Addict's Wife

Whether you are an experienced cruiser, or in the dreaming-about-it stage, you'll enjoy **Tips From The Cruise Addict's Wife**. *Besides being crammed with more tips and hints than you'll find anywhere else, including how to save money, be the smartest passenger on any ship, and plan a great vacation, this acclaimed book is loaded with tips and stories that will have you laughing aloud.*

How To Complain...and get what you deserve

A customer's guide to complaining effectively in this day and age when customers feel like the low man on the totem pole.

Quick and Clever Kids' Crafts

Loaded with easy, classy crafts for children and adults. A must for parents, teachers, scout leaders and anyone else who'd rather see a creative child than a bored one

Awesome Science Experiments for Kids

Simple, impressive science experiments; a fun teaching tool for adults to share with kids

Savory Mug Cooking

Easy-yet-impressive lunch recipes made with fresh ingredients, cooked right in your favorite mug! Expensive Take Out lunches—not anymore!

Uncommon Household Tips

Use ordinary items in extraordinary ways

Dozens of new uses for twenty ordinary household items you don't think twice about. From using golf tees to hang your hammer to dental floss for scrapbooking, you'll be inspired to look around the house before you run back to the store.

Made in the USA
Charleston, SC
17 March 2014